PROMISES
PROMISES

BY DOUGLAS MAXWELL

2010 TOUR

3-6 FEB	TRON THEATRE, GLASGOW
11 FEB	EASTWOOD PARK THEATRE, GIFFNOCK
12 FEB	CUMBERNAULD THEATRE, CUMBERNAULD
13 FEB	CARNEGIE HALL, DUNFERMLINE
17 FEB	THE LEMON TREE, ABERDEEN
18 FEB	BYRE THEATRE, ST ANDREWS
19 FEB	MACROBERT, STIRLING
20 FEB	HOWDEN PARK CENTRE, LIVINGSTON
23 FEB	PAISLEY ARTS CENTRE, PAISLEY
25-27 FEB	TRAVERSE THEATRE, EDINBURGH
2-13 MAR	SOHO THEATRE, LONDON
18-19 MAR	HARBOUR ARTS CENTRE, IRVINE
24 MAR	EDEN COURT THEATRE, INVERNESS
25 MAR	WOODEND BARN, BANCHORY

In association with Tron Theatre.

TRON
THEATRE

RANDOMACCOMPLICE

Random Accomplice are Scottish Theatre's top-notch touring patter merchants. Formed by Julie Brown and Johnny McKnight in 2002 we aim to entertain and make, you, the audience sit up and pay attention by telling you stories that make you gasp, giggle and greet.

Julie and Johnny have been described in the national press as "brilliant", "gifted" and "fiercely accessible."

"...demonstrates a healthy playfulness towards dramatic form and a lively curiosity about theatrical expression... "
The Guardian

Reviews of *Promises Promises*

"such sustained brilliance... it sometimes threatens to take the breath away... performed with an intensity, an allure, and a technical brilliance that is beyond praise... a story never to be forgotten"
The Scotsman

"Joanna Tope's performance is a tour de force... relentlessly unsettling and refuses to give simple answers to complex problems"
The Stage

"a fearless exploration of a modern liberal dilemma... highly accomplished."
Sunday Herald

Board of Directors
Andy Arnold (*Artistic Director, Tron Theatre*)
Julie Brown
Jane Davidson (*Director of Education, Scottish Opera*)
Marianne McAtarsney (*National Theatre Scotland Audience Development Manager*)
Andrew McKinnon (*Programme Director, Birbeck University*)
Johnny McKnight
Ruth Ogston (*Trust Fundraising Manager, Scottish Opera*)

Thanks to our Sponsors:

CAST & CREATIVE TEAM

Written by	Douglas Maxwell
Directed by	Johnny McKnight
Produced by	Julie Brown
Performed by	Joanna Tope
Set & Costume Design by	Lisa Sangster
Music composed by	Karen MacIver
Lighting Design by	Dave Shea
Video Design by	Tim Reid
Production Manager	Dave Shea
Stage Manager	Kay Hesford
Stage Manager	Gary Morgan
Press & Marketing Manager	Jane Hamilton
Graphic Design	Dave Pablo
Video Animation Trailer	Jamie MacDonald
Set Construction by	J & B Scenery

Thanks to:

Kirsty Paton Shea
Shona Miller
Kirsten Hogg
The Arches
Niall Walker
Severine Wyper, Eleanor Scott
and Matthew Lenton at
Vanishing Point Theatre
Company
CPE Lighting
Roy Fairhead
Ian Dow at Platform
Scottish Youth Theatre
Lucy Gaizley, Gary Gardiner &
Lyla Gaizely-Gardiner
Ellen Ling (RSAMD Placement Student)
and to Malcolm Rogan, Jo
Masson, David Sneddon and all
the staff at the Tron Theatre.

Special thanks to the board of Random Accomplice.

BIOGRAPHIES

Julie Brown – Producer

Trained The Royal Scottish Academy of Music and Drama. For Random Accomplice Accomplice credits include: Co-Devising & Performance of *Nothing To Fear Anymore, Intermission, Something Wicked, Seven Year Itch*. Director of *Little Johnny's Big Gay Musical, Cinderella* and co-director on *Marymassacre*. Producer of *Little Johnny's Big Gay Adventure, Marymassacre* and *Promises Promises*. Julie recently directed *Little Red Riding Hood* for the Arches and in Summer 2009 was the Project Manager for *Transform Caithness*, a National Theatre Scotland production. She also worked for 3 years as the Arches Education & Audience Development Officer.

Jane Hamilton – Press and Marketing Manager

Jane Hamilton is a Press and Marketing consultant who has just finished working on David Leddys award winning shows *White Tea and Susurrus* at the Edinburgh Fringe 2009. She previously worked as a writer and section editor for The List magazine before setting up her own business specialising in press, publicity and promotion. Working for various arts organisations in Scotland she has provided press and marketing support for theatre, film, galleries and other organisations including Scotland's Theatre Gateway, Theatre Cryptic, Vanishing Point Theatre Company and Playwrights Studio Scotland. She carried out the hugely successful press campaign for the launch of Black Camel Productions feature film Outpost (Sony 2009). She is also the Press Advisor for the Cultural Enterprise Office in Scotland.

Kay Hesford – Stage Manager

Since graduating from the University of Glasgow in Theatre, Film and Television, Kay has worked for numerous companies, as an ASM for Suspect Culture (*Casanova, Lament*), DSM for the Tron (*Possible Worlds* and *Jack and the Beanstalk*) and macrobert (*Mother Goose, Sleeping Beauty*). She has stage-managed for a number of companies including Random Accomplice, Paragon Ensemble, Gilmorehill G12 and Tall Stories. She was also the Technical Administrator at Gilmorehill G12 for 3 years. She was Production Manager for *Bard in the Botanics* and for the *FebFest* children's festival at macrobert last year. She recently completed two tours with Magnetic North, with After Mary Rose and Walden as Technical Stage Manager.

Karen MacIver – Composer

Karen studied composition for film at the Ealing Studios in London in 1996-97. She has written music for theatre and dance round the UK and had 7 theatre works performed last year including the score for Dundee Reps production of *Beauty & The Beast*, Scottish Opera's *Aunty Janet Saves The Planet* and the orchestral score for *A Head of Steam* – part of Homecoming Scotland.

Karen has been working with Matthew Lenton over the Christmas season, composing the music for *Snow Queen*. For Random Accomplice, Karen has composed the sound tracks for *Something Wicked, Cinderella, Marymassacre* and the live score for *Little Johnny's Big Gay Musical*.

Douglas Maxwell – Writer

Douglas Maxwell was born in 1974 in Girvan, a small town on the Ayrshire coast of Scotland. He is the author of many plays including *Decky Does A Bronco, Our Bad Magnet, Variety, If Destroyed True, Backpacker Blues, Melody* and *The Ballad of James II*. His work for young people includes Helmet, Beyond (with Nicola McCartney), *Mancub* and *The Mother Ship*. *The Mother Ship* won the Brian Way Award for best play for a younger audience, 2009.

He has also worked as Dramaturg with companies and artists such as Highway Diner, Lung Has, East Glasgow Youth Theatre, Giant Productions, David Leddy, Alan Bissett and Random Accomplice. His plays have been performed in translation in Germany, Norway, Hong Kong, New York, Chicago, Holland, Sweden and South Korea, where *Our Bad Magnet* completed a three year run.

Future productions in 2010 include *Promises Promises* for Random Accomplice; a musical for Cumbernauld Theatre called *The Bookie* and a major production with the National Theatre of Scotland entitled *The Miracle Man* directed by Vicky Featherstone. He is also writing a new play for young people for the National Theatre UK's "New Connections" project 2010. His play *Decky Does A Bronco* will also be remounted by Gridiron to mark its tenth anniversary.

His plays are published by Oberon Books and he is represented by St John Donald, United Agents Ltd.

Douglas Maxwell currently lives in Glasgow with his wife, Caroline Newall and his daughter Ellis.

Johnny McKnight – Director

Johnny trained at Royal Scottish Academy of Music and Drama. He works across arts practices as a writer, director, performer and educator. He has developed and delivered a multitude of projects for a range of organisations that include: macrobert, National Theatre of Scotland, Royal Scottish Academy of Music and Drama, Scottish Opera, Glasgow University, Scottish Opera, Scottish Youth Theatre, Langside College, North Ayrshire Council, Visible Fictions, Arches Theatre Company and 7:84 Theatre Company.

Gary Morgan – Stage Manager

Gary is working with Random Accomplice for the first time although he has previously worked with Mr McKnight and Miss Brown on various projects. Recent work includes *Sleeping Beauty* (macRobert), *Hare and Tortoise* (Licketyspit) and *Transform Caithness* (National Theatre Scotland)

Lisa Sangster – Set & Costume Designer

Lisa trained at the Royal Welsh College of Music and Drama. Previous work for Random Accomplice includes *Little Johnny's Big Gay Musical* on tour and *Cinderella* with the Byre Theatre. Other design credits include – *The Snow Queen* (Carnegie Hall), *Curse of the Demeter* (Visible Fictions), *Transform Dumfries* (National Theatre Scotland Learn), *Baby Baby* (Stellar Quines/Perissology), *Carthage Must Be Destroyed* (Ustinov Studio, Bath), *Sixteen* (Arches Theatre Co.), *The Pearlfisher; strangers, babies; Broke, Distracted,*

White Point (Traverse), *A Walk in the Park; Tir nan Og* (Oran More, Edinburgh Festival 2007) *The Patriot* (Tron) *Tartuffe* (Royal Welsh College of Music & Drama), *Hambledog and the Hopping Clogs* (Perissology Theatre Productions), *A Solemn Mass for a Full Moon in Summer* (Bigwood Productions). Design Consultant for *Lamb to the Slaughter* (Grid Iron Theatre Co.).

Dave Shea – Production Manager and Lighting Designer

Dave has worked in Scottish Theatre for 13 years as a Lighting Designer, Production Manager and Technical Manager. After 4 enjoyable years as Production Manager of 7:84 Theatre Company Dave left to pursue freelance opportunities which saw him work with the likes of National Theatre Scotland, Sounds of Progress, Suspect Culture, East Glasgow Youth Theatre and Random Accomplice.

Dave has been Production Manager and Lighting Designer on *Something Wicked, Little Johnny's Big Gay Adventure* (twice!), *Little Johnny's Big Gay Musical* (twice!) and *Mary Massacre* (twice!) for Random Accomplice.

Dave has recently been Lighting Designer on *Monaciello* (Tron Theatre Company at Napoli International Festival), *Bette/Cavett* (Tangerine Productions), *Sleeping Beauty* (MacRobert Arts Centre), *Little Red*

Riding Hood (Arches), and Lighting Designer & Production Manager of *Santa's Little Helpers* for Tron Theatre Company.

Tim Reid – Video Design

Tim sees video as a creative tool which – like lighting and sound – can add atmosphere and wonder to a live performance. He enjoys finding ways to use video creatively, flexibly and reliably as part of a show. Tim has designed video effects and playback systems for shows from experimental small scale works up to full scale Opera and Drama productions. He has designed video for shows by Vox Motus, Dogstar, National Theatre of Scotland, Wee Stories, David Leddy, Theatre By The Lake, The Arches and TAG. He has recently worked as Head of Video for the National Theatre of Scotland and toured internationally as a Video Operator for DV8 Physical Theatre.

Joanna Tope – Actress

Joanna Tope obtained a degree in Drama at Manchester University under the watchful eye of Stephen Joseph, who invited her to join his Theatre in the Round Company in Scarborough where she created the role of Ginny in Alan Ayckbourns *Relatively Speaking*.

Ten years of non-stop work followed with seasons at Pitlochry, Lincoln Theatre Royal in Philip Hedleys renound company, Birmingham Repertory with Peter Dews, Manchester Stables Company and the Northcott at Exeter with Jane Howell.

Television credits at that time included *Emmerdale Farm, Z Cars, The Tomorrow People* and *Shadow of the Tower* and radio credits; *Northern Drift* and *A Horseman Riding By*.

Between *Bingo* at the Royal Court with Sir John Gielgud and *Glorious Miles* at The Crucible in Sheffield, Joanna visited her parents in Scotland, met and married a wonderful man and came to live in Glasgow. Three children (Tom, John and Maggie Service all now with careers in the Arts) followed and much work at the Citizens Theatre, including *Oedipus, A Taste of Honey Peer Gynt* and *Cheri*, The Royal Lyceum in Edinburgh in *Death of a Salesman, A Christmas Carol* and *Dangerous Liaisons*. She appeared in *Frozen* for Rapture Theatre and Wit for Stellar Quines.

Joanna's extensive radio work includes Book of the Week, Book at Bedtime, Short Stories, Afternoon plays and Classic Serials. She has also recorded for BBC Audio Books. Television credits at this time include *Monarch of the Glen* and *The Ruby Ring*.

This is Joanna's first time working with Random Accomplice about which she is tickled pink.

A NOTE FROM DOUGLAS MAXWELL (WRITER)

A year or so ago I was in the pub with some pals arguing about a documentary which had just been on Channel 4. John Snow had presented the programme which coyly argued that some immigrants are more beneficial to the UK than others. In the end there was a list, with Indians at the top and Somalis at the bottom.

There was a teacher at the table who told us a story about a recent personal experience with a Somali child in a school in London. It was a harrowing story and my jaw dropped. I could not believe that any school in Britain would sleepwalk into that situation in the name of, I suppose, cultural fairness.

Even after the conversation moved on I asked them to tell the story again. And then as we're leaving later that night, I asked for the story one more time.

My mum and dad were teachers. My dad was a nationally respected teacher and a very successful headmaster. Before he died he was often brought in as a consultant for failing schools. I wondered what he would've done in that situation. Easy, I thought. It wouldn't've happened. There's no story there.

But I wanted there to be a story. I wanted to tell it. I was in the middle of a stuttering re-write and was feeling a bit stuck. Very often at those times I find myself writing something else – something I dont send out or sell, something for free, something just for me. It gets me match-fit again and injects a bit of newness into the re-writes when I go back to them.

I decided I would write up the teacher's story, without notes or preparation and see what happened. For the story to exist at all I knew it couldn't be a young teacher who would flow along and recover, and I knew it couldn't be a great, powerful teacher who would nip the whole thing in the bud right from the start. So I thought of an older teacher who is also, somehow, fundamentally, powerless.

Her voice was very strong and the monologue flowed quickly

and brightly (these pieces I write for myself very often turn out to be monologues, its my natural form – dramatic, no-matter what anyone says, especially when the person talking would never *ever* speak these words aloud in real life). Bright, quickly flowing writing doesn't happen much in these parts so I was excited. I can't remember how long it took me to write the first draft, but it wasn't long. Week's rather than months. I seem to remember writing it over the Christmas holidays always surprised by the turns the story took and the way the story and images moved towards the inevitable, Gothic finale. I wrote it at our kitchen table, rather than in the converted cupboard I usually write in. It was written on a laptop Linda Mclean had given me rather than my normal machine. It felt good to be bunking off. It's important sometimes to slip away and write just for the sake of it – because you somehow must.

Random Accomplice had commissioned me upon hearing a casually-dropped hint in some key note speech or other that I had no work, no money and a baby on the way. It was a lifesaver, but the trouble was I couldn't come up with anything for them. Anything good anyway.

I had imagined a massive *Arabian Nights* thing with loads of comic stories flowing in and out of each other. It was to be called *Humbug* and would use all the half-done stories I had piled up in my notebooks over the years. The trouble was there was no point to it and everything I did therefore had the forced feeling of a B Side collection. There was no personal connection there at all. I didn't feel anything for the play. It had nothing to do with me.

It was horrible to stop after 4 or 5 months working on the piece but it had to be done. I felt bad that they were such a small company, whose work I loved and who were counting on the play. They weren't a big theatre with a roll of projects to shuffle through. So I contacted Julie and Johnny and we arranged a meeting. I also e mailed them *Promises Promises* as a kind of consolation prize. Really just so the e mail had an attachment and looked at first glance like I'd done what I said I'd do.

At the meeting they were amazing - understanding and

hilarious and perfectly calm. I was to take my time and see what happened. Almost as we were putting on our coats Johnny mentioned that he loved *Promises Promises*. The more he talked about it, about how it had made him feel and the ideas it inspired the more I thought that this should be the play. Okay it wouldn't be the popular comedy/typical Random show wed planned but in my experience good shows come from this initial impulse of passion and chance, not from pre-planned career moves.

So off they went, away to begin the no doubt difficult job of drumming up enthusiasm for a reading of *Promises Promises*. In the meantime, inspired by the freedom of no deadline or expectations I wrote a new play for them called *Cooper McGees Dad*. The reading convinced us that we were right – *Promises Promises* is the play we should do.

Sometimes I wonder what my personal connection to this story is. What makes me feel it so strongly – as much now as when I first heard the true version? Is it something to do with my teacher friend? Or my teacher mum...teacher aunt...teacher dad?

Or was it that my baby had been born and she was a little girl?

A NOTE FROM JOHNNY MCKNIGHT (DIRECTOR)

I can tell you exactly where I was when I first read the script for *Promises Promises*. I can tell you every detail. It was on the Virgin Train, it was a Friday, it was pouring of rain outside. I was wearing a black, knitted jumper and converse trainers. It was, for me, one of those moments that you remember – vividly. An email from Douglas was sitting in my in-box. At the time he was working on a script commission for Random Accomplice (called *Humbug*). In the email there was an early first act draft of *Humbug* and another attachment, entitled *Promises Promises*. Douglas said it was something that had been "sitting in his drawer" and wondered "what we thought of it."

40 minutes later I was on the phone to Julie. You have to read this. We need to do this. I need to do this. I've never read anything like it. This needs to be our next show, there's nothing like this around at the moment. We need to tell Douglas to let no-one else see it.

So we did. We asked him to keep that drawer locked. Until now…

PROMISES
PROMISES

Douglas Maxwell

PROMISES
PROMISES

OBERON BOOKS
LONDON

First published in 2010 by Oberon Books Ltd
521 Caledonian Road, London N7 9RH
Tel: 020 7607 3637 / Fax: 020 7607 3629
e-mail: info@oberonbooks.com
www.oberonbooks.com

A catalogue record for this book is available from the British
Library.

ISBN: 978-1-84943-064-7

Cover design by Niall Walker

—Ah. It's the Pride of Miss Jean Brodie!

I find this remark so dispiriting; so sickeningly dispiriting that it's all I can do not to hurt the man.

If it would in any way further the matter, I would gladly set about this cretin, right here in the playground with a hardback edition of Dame Muriel Spark, but I know in my heart it would be…as everything is in this place, an impotent gesture.

—Prime, I say.
—What's that Maggie love?
—Prime. The *Prime* of Miss Jean Brodie.
—Prime? Oop. Loose a mark! Must try harder! And he slaps his own wrist and makes what he must consider to be a comical face.

I am heroically holding in an impulse to point out that the very fact he's arriving in school *after* me, is in itself a cause for concern, let alone his general ignorance in the world of literature, when he pirouettes so we're shoulder to shoulder and, against my will, in cahoots.

He's young and fun you see. In case you missed it. We *play* together. This has been decided. He is a plastic, digital toy and I am made of paper and lace. I am dusty, attic bound and vulnerable. You can play with me but you must be careful. These are the roles he assigned us the moment I arrived in the school, before a word had even passed my lips, and for some reason those roles are inescapable now.

But this is not how I see myself. This is not what I am like. At all.

He announced yesterday that the others in the staff room consider me "venerable". I said nothing in reply.

Venerable I can live with. Vulnerable: never.

So I am someone who would perhaps intimidate a young, moronic, Headmaster if he were not, like our saviour here, a Pirouetting, Joke-Cracking, People-Managing genius. This is the point he is making you see. He wants you to know that you are being handled.

—And how's the week been? Any trouble? I heard raised voices on day one. Yeah, it can be a tricky group. Ester should be back within the week so it's not a prison sentence. Shout if you need the cavalry, okay?

And then, just as I'm drawing my breath like an arrow from a quiver, he nudges me, and we're playmates again,

—Hey, I've got something in here that might cheer you up, and he reaches for his inside pocket.

That there's something in there that will "cheer me up" I *sincerely* doubt.

With a flourish he produces... A copy of *The Daily Record*.

I maintain an expression of dignified abhorrence.

—I've read it, he says, as if he were talking about the complete works of Shakespeare.

The Head is, as he would say, "a fellow Scot". This particular scar he wears with pride. To listen to him you would think we were the only two Scots living in London. The only two Scots to have ever even *thought* of living in London.

The Daily Record! This is the worst type of pretension. That he maintains this as an image! This grubby, kid-on illiterate, man-of-the-people rubbish. It occurs to me that he must go out of his way to track down this rag for moments such as these and for a second I actually pity him.

—It'll remind you of home eh?

I take it from him as one would take a paper handkerchief from a child and when he's a pace away I drop it in the bin.

Yes it does. It reminds me of home.

He spins.

–Oh Maggie, I need to see you about the new intake. It's sensitive so we'd better have a tête-à-tête in the batcave yeah? Quickly, before the second bell yeah?

And now from the end of the corridor, the shine from the floor in the pouring, primary school light, making him seem like some kind of religious vision...

–Prime? Are you sure it's Prime? Wouldn't Pride make more sense?

The bell is his answer.

And as I watch these swarming Untutored...these grabbing Unloved...these unwashed, unbreakable, unspeakable little Tragedies, bounce from me, like I was the bell and they were the sound, I think to myself...

Not always. Pride does not always make more sense.

***

My father handed me his pride like an heirloom.

I can feel him in my frame right now. The way my chin juts and my arms fold across my chest seem to be a horrible impersonation of the man. So I shift my body and move my face, try to find a new shape.

But more than that, it's the scrape of superiority in my throat that truly conjures up the spirit of my father, quicker than any séance ever could.

You see...I have never read *The Prime of Miss Jean Brodie*. I can only distantly remember the film. Maggie Smith's preposterous accent is all that remains. That and the wisecracks which have followed me from school to school.

So who am I to look down on this man, this Gordon Ottoway?

He has risen to a promoted post in education: I never did.

He can talk to people on many different levels: I can not.

For all I know he *has* read the novel and was making a joke that I missed because I was sneering and judging and fighting off the headache and…

Well.

My father was a tailor. He cut us from a hard, thorn-proof cloth that will never wear down to a comfortable fit.

My father was a tailor and he cut us alright.

So I'll be different in the office. I shall be bright and I shall be open.

I'll leave my father's pride behind. Leave him here in his dark, three piece, Easter Sunday suit and his scrubbed red Easter face and I shall be a different person. Play a different role.

To get into character I walk the corridor with my hips swaying and my heels clicking. I can still get looks when I walk. It's not the detail, it's the movement. It's the rhythm and it's the angles. A single woman of my age has to sway her way out of other people's definitions.

Click click click…

I am not a dry, church-going, cat-adoring member of a committee, whose only surge is to be found in a Dobey's tea room.

Click click click

My hips tell people that I am something else. My clothes are expensive, my jewellery sparkles and my shoes are impossible. Wives will coo about my style, but secretly,

I suppose, they take me as an insult. Husbands' eyes still linger of course.

I wear my sexuality like a holster. A low slung weapon.

I remember seeing a western when I was a girl. My sister and I saw it three times on a loop. We were hiding in that gargantuan cinema, terrified to go back to the shop. Montgomery Clift was a gunslinger whose pistols where hanging on his hips so low I thought he would never be able to reach the trigger. The belt cut across his crotch, shifting as he swaggered. His fingers swung loose and gigantically above us on the front row. Joan whispered in my ear, her breath like smoky, aniseed winter sweets, whispered…that she wanted to kiss him. This was a confession I think.

But I wanted to *be* him. The sway he had. I wanted the sex that was held low in that holster. So whenever I've wanted to stop pianos mid flow, I picture those pistols and I sway. There was a time in my life when this walk would guarantee that I'd get company.

And it occurs to me, as I catwalk the corridor that I can remember no specific details of any of the men I've ever slept with. Nothing at all.

I remember who they were of course. Most of them. I suppose. But as to details... it's a blank. I have no memories of their skin, their movements, their bodies, the sweat and the hair and the words they said or even how it *felt*. You'd think some of that would stick.

I wonder how many of those men are dead now? Must be a good number. Some will have died in the arms of the women they loved. I'd be a bitter taste to those I suppose. A mistake from the past. A lesson learned. But maybe I was the one for some? The one they wanted to lie with forever? It's possible. There were a few who fell for me. I remember their letters. But I can't remember their bodies.

Which is strange because I was good at sex. When you're defined by something you'd better be good at it.

And again, just before I rap the door of the Headmaster's office…my father. This time it's his disgust I feel. The revulsion at something he saw flicker across my twelve year old face. Or maybe it was a move in my body. The way I walked was it? The way I sat at the tea table with my legs crossed and my new red shoe dangling from my toe? But whatever it was, he saw it.

Not in Joan though.

He didn't see it in her. He made sure of that.

***

There is a sign on the desk that says "I've Told You Once, Call Me Gordon".

I won't be doing that. All my good intentions have drained away in the face of this drivel and I'm back to righteous indignation and barely suppressed rage.

My chin is jutted, my arms are crossed.

The Head has been joined at his desk by a woman in a mushroom coloured, dog-haired suit straight from Primark, who has yet to identify herself and is somehow under the impression I know absolutely nothing about everything.

I'm trying to work out what else she may have assumed. That I'm unable to teach the "children of today"? That I don't read the newspapers? Oh and of course, that I'm a racist. That goes without saying.

Her tone is that of a mother explaining to a rather slow child the dangers of electricity…

–The situation over there is very different when it comes to education and childcare in particular, so we do need to be *careful* about so many things. What we may consider

24

adequate methods of support are new to them and we need to *carefully* welcome her into the system whilst *carefully* reassuring her community that we don't want to sever what are, in the end, important cultural and historical practices.

I've taught for 40 years. I've taught in London for 35 of those. I have taught children from every corner of the globe and had every hue of skin imaginable beam back at me from behind those little desks. And, although I can't be sure, I would guess that the class *already* contains children from Somalia, so I'm at a complete loss as to the point of this patronising little lecture.

These are the moments when I remember why I retired. It doesn't happen often. Only when dealing with fellow teachers it has to be said.

My throat goes dry and for a moment I go faint for the craving.

I think of the flask in my bag and relax a bit.

I've retired twice now. Once from this very school, and again from that short lived disaster up in Scotland. This time I am back to cover a sick leave. No-one is queuing up for this job. I live ten minutes from the gate. The secretary, Mrs Haan, came to my door with a bag of apples.

The mushroom is still talking…

—And also, for some of the class, this could be an interesting part of their cultural development. Halloween is coming up so perhaps it can be *carefully* folded into some kind of long term project? Perhaps a project is an idea mmm? Might let you reign back some control? Mr Ottoway says there were raised voices on day one.

Right that's enough of this dowdy cow. I raise my finger and she is silenced. This is a skill a teacher develops through time. The finger then points at "I've Told You Once Call Me Gordon".

—You, I say. Explain, in a clear voice, what she is talking about and why it affects myself or my class in the tiniest way.

He sits upright. Nearly blushes, but stops himself somehow. As he does so I catch a flash of some male incident in his face. But then he remembers the roles, and smiles.

—Oh my. Yes miss no miss! Absolutely. Ha! Ha! Well Maggie. The girl in question...

—For the moment we're calling her Rosie.

—Right, Rosie, will be in your class this morning yeah?

—I am aware of this. I was informed of the girl's arrival on day one. I was told she spoke English and that she would...

—Yeah, em, yeah. See this morning it won't just be the girl though, she'll have with her...

He indicates that the Mushroom is the only one qualified to continue this sentence. So she does. Carefully...

—At about 11, a community leader and some others will be popping in to perform a short ceremony, with the girl, as part of an ongoing rite she's involved in. A ritual. Mmm?

I feel queasy even at the phrase "community leader". In my experience it often means the exact opposite.

—A ritual? In *my* classroom?
—In Ester's classroom actually Maggie. This wouldn't be an issue with a...
—With a younger teacher? Is that what you were going to say? A younger teacher would be *delighted* at having a new child introduced to Year Two surrounded by a tribe of God knows who, doing God knows what for a whole morning, is that it?

Yes, we are all aware that I used the word "Tribe".

—I was going to say, it wouldn't be an issue with a teacher who would be with the girl for the entire school year and could help her adjust through time. If you like, myself or Poppy-Sue…

Poppy-Sue! For God sake.

—…Can be with you when the party arrive yeah.

I stand to my full height and then sink slightly onto one hip, letting Poppy-Sue and "I've Told You Once Call Me Gordon" see exactly what they're dealing with here.

She steals a glance at my shoes, and he at my chest.

—No assistance required thank you very much.

I'm at the door and turn, more for the drama than for the information…

—And what, pray tell, is the exact "ritual" my class and I are to be carefully folding into a long term project?

They look at each other before he answers.

—Rosie is…an Elective Mute. It means…

—I can work out what it means Mr Ottoway thank you very much. And these "community leaders" are going to make her talk is that it? Well, that should be very interesting.

—Eh, well, actually, we need to be *careful* because it's more complicated than that, mmm? You see within Rosie's community and more importantly, her immediate family, there is some concern, a very *real* concern actually, that the fact she is *choosing* not to speak means she is…well… possessed.

—Possessed?

—Mmm.

—Possessed by what?

—By…devils.

I believe she's saying something about being careful when I slam the door.

***

Devils!

They're actually allowing...no...*inviting*...inviting these people through the gates and into my classroom. It literally stuns me. I can feel the dull ricochet of this stupidity tingle on my face.

And of course there will be a political motivation somewhere behind this lunacy. Oh of course! Some accusation in the papers that must be refuted; something bubbling in the alleys of the catchment area that must be cooled. Some...some good intention that's been crowded into by some other good intention and some more and some more until it's a mob of good intentions rampaging, destroying everything in its wake.

Take a deep breath Margaret Ann. Count to ten.

1-2-

Is this really any worse than what was announced yesterday? That the forty thousand pound budget for the year had been spent on laptop computers. Do devils and exorcisms really make less sense than that?

3-4

No books. At all. For the whole school.

5

In my classroom...sorry...in Ester's classroom, there is one shelf of books. Dictionaries. And not English dictionaries. English to Russian, English to French, English to God knows what.

6

I teach six year olds. They're only six years old.

***

My hand pauses, as it always does, on the handle of the classroom door.

If a teacher doesn't feel the slightest rush of…well maybe not nerves…but of *ignition*, before they enter the classroom first thing in the morning then they should go while the going's good.

I did.

The children are lined up. I straighten my back and they go quiet. Some things, when dealing with younger children, need no dictionary.

They file in happily. They are happy to be at school. This will not last. And that is natural. But for now it is our job to harness this happiness and to live up to the promise it implies.

As always at this point in the day, I think of Wendy.

In my first school, the famous Wendy Malloy of Red Street, said that teaching was all about living up to a promise. I don't know who said it first, but it was Wendy who said it to me.

Everything Wendy wore she had sewn herself on her Mother's Singer, and it seemed to me, a slightly younger woman, that she had also sewn together her ideas, her words, her very *being*, on that old pedal machine. For all those wonderful things Wendy said; about life, education, politics, women; they were familiar, traceable, gathered from other people's scraps, but they always seemed to fit her so well. She'd trimmed away what didn't suit, until the words were skin tight. She spoke straight from the dressing up box and I was truly educated in those lunch hours listening to her.

And then one day she was gone.

We had walked arm in arm through the Saturday cinema crowds, week in week out. Then one Wednesday there was a note left on my step, taped to the top of a parcel, saying she had met a man and was leaving for London to be with him. She had met him on her trip to Russia.

A man I'd never heard of. Not one word of.

We were extremely close, she and I. Like sisters.

So…Wendy…Wendy said a child comes to school because they've been promised that here is where they will learn all they need to know. So all *we* have to do is follow up on that promise. In tiny drops.

Day by day, hour by hour, page by page.

Every day, tell them *exactly* what will be taught between now and the bell, and then you do it. Simple. Live up to that promise every day, for each and every child. In tiny drops.

I saw her once at the buffet of a union conference in the late 1970s. She had become one of those dreaded women. Nothing to say now. Her outfit was ill-fitting. She was unrecognisable actually. Her husband was an unlovable keynote speaker, she was on his arm. He, a fat, bald man with a look about him of vests and stinking feet. She, someone who had given up teaching to have a baby.

I was very pleasant to her.

And regardless of what she did, I think of her every morning as the children file in and stand by their chairs, believing with their whole heart that promises will always be kept.

This will not last either.

And that's natural too.

***

It's only as I turn to follow the children into the classroom that I see her standing there.

Her back is pressed into the wall, the coats on their hooks bulging around her like a tangled parachute.

Her eyes meet mine directly.

And…I feel…something shift.

There's a steadiness in her gaze that makes me feel accused, and I straighten instinctively against it.

She is not hiding. Her head is not bowed. Her eyes are not wide or teary. Her lip is not petted, or quivering. She doesn't cling to her schoolbag for the memory of her mother. No, she does none of these things.

She just steadily holds my gaze. And I'm aware that I have missed my moment of authority.

But still the gaze goes on. Gaze into stare, stare into… something else.

I feel like I've discovered an old photograph of myself that I didn't know existed, and I'm studying it, studying it, studying it. Can't take my eyes from it. Trying to fit a time and a place to this snapshot. Studying the clothes and the hair and the light, trying to fit this new piece of evidence into the gospel of my memory.

Is that really me?

No. Of course it's not.

There are no similarities.

Hair is wire-scraped and bound. Skin as black and hard as a bomb. Her eyes, hooded, but not insolent, are the ivory of a label on a bottle of poison.

She's not smiling.

And although her arms are crossed and her chin is jutted, she is a world away from me, so it can't be that which has us locked in this ridiculous gunfighters silence.

And her red shoes…well…they are nothing like mine.

—You look like your name is…Rosie? Is it?

She holds my eye, but doesn't react.

I put my foot next to hers.

—We both have on red shoes. Do you know what that means? It means we like the same things. So I wonder if it also means I can guess how you *feel* too? Shall I try? Maybe you can tell me when I get it wrong? I guess that…you feel butterflies in your tummy. I guess that…you feel out of place here. I guess that you think that you're all on your own. And I guess that you want to go home?

Something ripples across her face. That will do.

I hold out my hand. She doesn't take it.

—Rosie, my name is Miss Brodie, and in my classroom you'll learn everything you need to know. And nothing bad can happen to you in my classroom because I will always be there. That is a promise. Do you know what a promise is?

She nods.

A match is struck inside me.

—I'm going to turn around now and go into the classroom, where we'll be learning and playing and making friends. I want you to watch my shoes when I walk, and when you're ready, I want you to follow in my footsteps. Put *your* red shoes where *my* red shoes have been and all will be well. Do you believe me? Rosie, do you believe me?

And finally…another nod.

—Good girl. Then let us walk.

I feel like a gymnast beginning a floor routine as I slowly turn and walk back towards the classroom door.

Step by step…away from her.

She doesn't move.

I can see her silhouette, reflected in the dark glass of a framed certificate.

Come on girl. Follow me. Follow me!

I will not break stride. I will not turn.

Follow me.

Follow me.

Please.

I'm at the door when she makes her first move. Pulled towards me. So that's the distance is it? That's the length of the cord that binds us together.

I turn to watch her now, I'm holding the door and was planning to smile, but instead my mouth hangs open.

She's walking towards me, her footsteps in mine.

But more than that…she has copied my walk, my gait, my entire bearing…*exactly*.

Her hips swing, her chin juts, her fingers are loose and low, swishing the air. It would be a mocking thing, a horrible thing, if she wasn't so intensely focused on her role. So transformed.

Empowered by the being of me.

Something in my heart burns. A quick, singe of…pain.

Like a match flaring up for the last time, before it goes out.

***

I place Rosie on the table pushed against mine which luckily contains a little boy called Brian who has a tendency to cry. This is natural, and is a sign of intelligence and compassion in little boys and will fade as he gets older. But for now, he'll be a sound companion for her. I can see that he is already showing her a pencil case that he's especially proud of.

Good.

I move Lee to the back of the class, which he takes as a promotion. There was a time when you kept your eye on children called Lee. Lees tended towards the troublesome. Now it seems to be ones who share their names with holiday destinations who are most likely to act out.

My headache is clearing. My throat is dry but in a thirsty way. I can live with thirst. I like it. It leads to something.

Rosie's table, by sheer chance, also contains another girl who I have always presumed to be Somali although there doesn't seem to be any immediate rapport. Quite the opposite actually. But then again, myself and Call Me Gordon both come from the same country and rapport isn't exactly on the cards there either.

I introduce Rosie, and those who understand chant back a heartfelt welcome.

I'm about to move on when I remember the impending... ceremony.

–And we will also be having a visitor later this morning, and I want you all to be on your best behaviour. It will be very interesting for everyone I'm sure and will be a lovely way for us to welcome Rosie to the class.

My words hang in the air like the lie it is and it strikes me again that this is preposterous. If they consider it absolutely vital that this "community leader" deals with devils, then he will do so in the nurses room and *not* in front of my children.

Full Stop.

The girl is looking at me now, neither as a friend nor a traitor. But as a sporting opponent, waiting with interest to see my next move.

I share her curiosity.

***

The rest of the morning we continue with the week's work. I have abandoned the plan left by the absent Ester as it was inappropriate. Her ambitions for this class manage to simultaneously underestimate the children, and flummox them.

She has nursery-level worksheets mixed with written work that isn't especially useful to a child who cannot read English. I for one do not equate a skill in foreign languages with intelligence in a six year old.

So, instead, we are doing integrated work on the subject of Autumn. We've done seasons, tree names and an adding and subtracting exercise based on falling conkers. We've had Halloween drama, after which I recited "Tam o' Shanter", which transcends language. Which is lucky, considering it is written in one which no-one actually speaks. But it captured them, as it always has, with rhythm, sound and spirit. The "raised voices" our glorious leader heard in the corridor on day one were spontaneous cries of terror and encouragement for Tam, as poor Meg raced towards that bridge, her tail ripped from her by evil spirits as she bolts for home.

Today we are to be making leaves from an ancient roll of brown velvet I have dragged in from the house. The material is all that remains of an attempt I made to summon the spirit of Red Street and be the God of my own wardrobe. Perhaps I was trying to save money or something, I can't remember; but when the material arrived, its sheer *brownness* robbed me of any good intentions I may have had – it was shoved under the bed untouched and I was in Selfridges within the hour.

I've also brought in my father's tailoring tools which was a mistake on all counts.

They are stiff, ancient things, wrapped in chamois. Precious hand-me-downs they are not. I took them from their hooks in his shed, leaving their painted outline on the wall like a crime scene and flung them into my bag on the night when I finally fled his house. Not as a memento. But rather as a slap in his face. Something he would discover missing only after time and hopefully feel a pang or two when he did. I stole them, for the joy of stealing, nothing else. He didn't mourn them I'm sure. His business was gone and his hands shook by that time anyway. I'm not sure if he even went out to the shed in those last few years.

But still, the very sight of those wooden handles inspire a good deal of guilt in me. An unjust guilt.

After all, we have agreed, he was the guilty one.

When I brought out the tailoring scissors and began cutting the rough, leaf-shaped slabs for the children to fold and glue, I am aware that my mistake with these things runs deeper than any bad memory they may inspire. The tailoring scissors are shears really. His favourite. He called them The Persuader, and he kept the thing in his trouser pocket as he worked, where they bulged ridiculously. They are long, extended blades in stiff grips which are completely inappropriate for a room crammed with curious six year olds with slippery fingers.

I know too, that this type of error is exactly what Call Me Gordon would be expecting from me. Either that or…well, put it this way, a dusty arsenal of deadly weapons won't help my cause.

I stuff them in my bag and kick it under my desk.

Within an hour though, the class has noticed Rosie's silence and it is that, rather than The Persuader, which starts to cut their attention.

It's not just silence. She refuses to interact.

No nods now, no mime, no gesture.

She is a silent *nothing*. She is a void, whose gravity pulls all the other children into its dark wee orbit of quiet.

Except when addressed directly by me that is.

Oh she will acknowledge me.

A small shake of the head or a shrug being the peak of communication.

I try to think back to our moment in the corridor. What was it I said there to win her trust, if indeed that is what I've done? There wasn't anything.

Was there?

But somehow she feels, we *both* feel I suppose, that a connection was made.

As I watch her carefully but cluelessly fold that brown cloth, I can't shake the…irrational…feeling that she is…in some way…

Me.

The bell rings for break and as the others go, Rosie stays seated until I tell her she should run along and play.

Her first few steps to the door have that holster swinging swagger I know so well.

–Don't do that!

She drops her head and shuffles out.

–Walk…walk properly please.

I shouldn't've…I was too hard there.

I have to seriously fight the instinct to run after her. To physically shield her against the mortars and horror of being new in a playground. Does any terror in life really compare to being new in a playground?

Not many.

***

The temperature of the room has been forced up like an old window, shuddered up dangerously to a hothouse boom and the air pressure makes reason impossible.

We seem packed in now, shoved to the corners. A buzz of headache static hovers over the desks and wrinkles the paper of the drawings on the wall.

My desire to huckle these people into the nurses' room was dismissed with a wave of the Headmaster's hand as if I have made the same demand on a daily basis for years.

And anyway, my priority now is control.

Brian wept as soon as they walked in of course, but even Lee seems shaky and on the edge of something now. The children are holding each other and I can only be physically reassuring to three or four at a time, so I move constantly, cuddling and touching, whispering wee warm words in their ears as I flit.

That the Headmaster doesn't see the effect this is having, that he's either ignoring it in the face of some political compromise, or is simply blind to it, makes me wish him dead.

He is not fit to be in charge of children. Not fit.

He stands by the board; flaccid, pink, small, gripping an A4 pad with both hands. His eyes, like all eyes, are magnetized by what is happening to Rosie.

At first, of course, I protested. I put my arm around her and swore refusal; hips, eyes, words blazing.

But as we argued, the class grew worried, restless, scared and…and a border had then been crossed and my decision was made for me.

I made my class a promise after all.

And then it was too late. They had started.

There are three of them. Two women, in their early twenties I would say. Acolytes. Wrapped in dazzling sheets of colour and the self satisfied air of the bloody minded. I can see in their tutting and amused condescension that they are of the breed of ignoramus who consider everyone else in the world to be stupid.

They do nothing. Occasionally they mouth responses and whisper agreements but really I can see no function in their appearance except as spectators, accusers, witnesses to this.

The man however, is busy.

He is the star. He is the priest of this fiasco. A fat boy in his late to middle age, his robes are stretched over an arrogant belly and he stinks of perspiration and clothes picked up from a bedroom floor. He wears dress black leather shoes, made more visible by the light, African, man-made fibre of the rest of his outfit.

His belief in his own greatness is the battery behind this performance. He is a man I imagine, surrounded by woman who adore him. He will speak in monologue at the kitchen tables of the world. His opinion is the last word. His decisions will be greeted by shaken heads of amazement, stunned by his brilliance.

His voice is round and well practised, full of the surprising switches of pace and stretched pronunciation that draws out vowels and syncopates syllables in a way I usually find so pleasing, but seems so vile in the here and now.

He is, in short, a religious man.

And God, I recognize him.

And Rosie…

Well. Wee Rosie…

Rosie has been told to stand by her desk as he runs his hands over her invisible shield and sings snatches of something which has the ring of made up gibberish, regardless of language.

I hear "zav" I hear "wadaddo".

Rosie is completely still. Rosie is not here. I want to know where she is.

Where does she go to save herself from this? Because she seems so untroubled. A girl who is not in use. Like a marionette hooked to a stand, she hangs there, ready for life when it comes, but now…nothing.

And yet…she is only six years old! She is in a new class and she has to be the focus of this…this…*disgrace.*

Does she believe them then? These horrible, dangerous, fools.

She must. She must believe herself to be possessed by spirits or…

But why won't she speak, why not clear her name? No. If she wanted to, she could.

I would, so she would.

So either she can't – is psychologically forbidden somehow

Or she has *decided* on silence.

Yes. That's it. That's what is happening. This little girl has decided that silence is the only way.

In all this sound, in this cacophony of blind and selfish nonsense, in the terror of all these little eyes she has said to herself, "I will not speak" and I can't help but feel…pride.

Good for you wee Rosie. "Weel done Cutty Sark". You're the genius here. Not these people. Never them.

Louder it gets, louder.

Yelps from the acolytes and English from the master of ceremonies.

—Out of her! Out, you hear me, out now!

They're softly bouncing to some invisible rhythm and nodding as if this was the truest thing, as everything gets bigger, higher, bigger, higher.

And then she looks at me. Rosie. Eye to eye again. A new look now. Not anger, not disappointment, just a look of resignation:

There's nothing anyone can do. This is what the world is like.

He's still chanting at her, moving around her, sprinkling liquid from a bottle that smells like perfume and makes her blink.

—Out! he's saying. Out!

Yes. I recognize him.

I have thrown the French to English dictionary before I even realised I had picked it up. It hits him full in the face and one of the women has the cheek to scream.

I'm moving towards him, pistols drawn.

—I quite agree with you Sir. Out! Out! On you go. All of you!

The Head is flapping somewhere or other…

—Now Miss Brodie, we spoke about this yeah…

–I want you and your vampires out of this room immediately or I shall not be responsible for my actions. You are distressing this child and infecting the class with your ignorance which is absolutely unforgivable. You should be ashamed of yourself!

He has recovered from whatever impact the dictionary has made on his brain and stands to his full height. As do I.

His eyes travel down my body and he smiles as if to say that he has me all summed up. I'm one of *those* women. He is assuming of course, as men do, that my hatred is due to my uncontrollable sexual desire. He's even nodding as if to say he approves of it, he *likes* my fire. Before he can laugh in my face I'm pointing in his.

–Take yourself away from here and away from this child. I am going to make it my mission in life to have you prosecuted for this and if I see you in school again I will…

He puts out his hand and softly touches the skin on the inside of my wrist. It's a strange violation and I squirm.

He's smiling. Saying something to one of the women who laughs.

My fury is amazing. My father's pride. My father is right… right here. I have a stapler in my hand like a knife.

–You people have to learn. You people think you have the right to bring this here. This disease of folklore and superstition…

The head is grabbing my arm

– Miss Brodie…

–This preposterous abuse of adulthood in the name of religion, well unfortunately we educate children here…

–Miss Brodie

–…we *protect* children in this room, we fight for the right to deliver our promise!

–Miss Brodie step outside…

–She's done nothing wrong! Deal with me! You won't send her away! You hear me! You will not send her away! It's me you should deal with! Me!

There's a silence. Brian is crying. And so are some others. The priest, or whatever he is, is smiling. The women are shaking their heads, theatrically disgusted.

–What?

–Miss Brodie I am suspending you from teaching duties until a disciplinary committee can be…

–Wait a minute, what? You're suspending *me*? You can't suspend me.

–Racism cannot be tolerated…

–Racism? Oh don't be preposterous, I have a class to teach.

–Not today. Today you're going home. You clearly referred to our guests here as "you people" a slur which this school…

–I was talking about religious people Mr Ottoway.

–That…that…is the same if not worse…

–My father… My father was a religious man. I know what damage can be done if…

–Maggie. Go home. I was aware of your record, the incident in Scotland…

I feel faint now.

I fold my arms. I jut my chin.

–…and I was aware that taking you on, even for a few days was a risk and I'm afraid to say the gamble has backfired. Please leave the room. Mr em…Mr Wadad, you have my whole hearted apology for what just happened here and I can promise…

I don't hear his promise. I don't hear anything.

I walk out. Shakily.

A fallen gymnast.

A wounded cowboy.

A stupid old woman.

***

I stand by the sinks like a giant.

I am in the junior girls' toilets. I have to stoop to see my face in the little mirror, which I do only once. Instead, I lean my forehead against the tiles and let the coldness of the wall go through me.

There is a smell of bulk-bought disinfectant and brittle paper towels.

I left my bag in the classroom.

Then a bolt…

The flask is in there! I need that flask.

Every time. Every single time. The same mistake, over and over…

I say too much, too late and do nothing for the good.

I'm not a giant. I'm just in the wrong room.

I'm not better than these people. I'm just…I'm just…

I'm just my father's favourite.

And there's nothing I can do about that.

I was forgiven. Joan was punished.

I was the warning, Joan the reaction.

I stayed at home…and Joan was sent away.

She was to have a religious life, away from the sins I had brought into the house. He made it sound like he was punishing me and saving her. But it was the opposite of course.

She was to live her life in institutions one way or another. Bulk-bought disinfectant and brittle paper towels. Day in. Day out. And I was free to say too much, too late and do nothing for the good.

I was just coming home…at about 7 in the morning. Rounding the corner of Ailsa Street East, bare feet, heels in hand and my red party dress loose around me. I could've been naked for all the difference it made.

And there they were. My family at the gate. At first I was delighted. Father would roar at me now. With this disgrace the spell would break. I'd sensed his disgust for a year, his leer even, at the way I was, at the things I did. At the things I would get him to do. But here now, was the proof.

I was a stop out. I was a hoor. I was bad in a way only girls could be. *I* was the bad one.

Now he could scream at me for once, and not at her.

Not wee Joan who still believed in God. And fathers.

Wee Joan that was…getting helped into the back of Mr Coal's car with my father's old suitcase jammed in beside her. Wee Joan's face at the back window hypnotised by the sight of me swaying down the street, as good as naked, heels in hand.

−What's happening? Where's Joan going?

He wouldn't even look at me.

–Joan's had the call. It's her vocation. She's to be looked after. Girls like her can be raised in the ways of light. It's for the best. Girl's like her…

Then he banged a palm on the roof of the car and away it went.

I ran. Right down the middle of the street I ran after her. She was waving all the way. She looked terrified. As Mr Coal's battered old motor coughed around that corner and pulled away, she looked terrified.

For the rest of her life she always looked terrified to me.

When I got back to the house my feet were bleeding. I trailed blood red footprints from the door, to the drinks cabinet, up the stairs to my room.

I should've left too. That very day. But I didn't. I stayed.

I stayed. I stayed silent.

And I drank.

And as I sit here on the floor of this doll's house loo, I can already see what the rest of the day holds. That old craving has never failed me. I can see me finishing the flask outside the gate, in full view of whoever. I can taste the vodka I'll buy from the corner shop that's not quite my local, but they'll know the order alright. I'm in there most days.

I can already feel the calm, slickness of the alcohol in my rib cage and the kindling in my stomach set alight sip by sip. I'll drink it from a shot glass stolen from a café in Moscow and smuggled back as a gift in a homemade dress by Wendy Malloy from Red Street. And left on my step with a note on top.

I'll start off sitting in my old arm chair, but will stand later when the drama gets me. And I'll be angry at first, replaying and re-enacting this morning's debacle, me cast in the role of the eloquent heroine, triumphant over the parade of fools who surround her. I'll do all the voices at top blast.

It'll be a monologue. Of course. Ornaments will be smashed.

And later I'll get it confused, then have it wiped away completely and I'll be blank again. It will all be jumbled and lost, garbled and then forgotten like the rest of me and I'll be the questing hero no more, but just a woman who does *nothing*. A woman who should've spoken sooner but didn't. A woman who should've done something…but didn't.

And I'll be drunk.

And I'll be….

I think I'm…I think I'm coming loose. I recognize the feeling. It's happened before.

Retirement number two. A tiny country school near to Joan. That was the plan. But she wouldn't see me at this point. Wouldn't even come to the gates to meet me. They said she was in prayer. No-matter when I visited. Prayer. But she wasn't. She was watching me from some high, stained glass window. I knew it. I felt her. Her wee eyes, old now, and full of blame. Terrified still. Of me.

I would shove my pathetic presents in the bin as I swayed away, each and every day.

I would drink before my visits, I would drink after my visits. Then there were no visits. But I would drink none the less.

Then it happened, out of nowhere. A cleaner…her crucifix; cheap gold and prominent. I watched her lazily push her mop under the tables of my classroom. This was early. No pupils. No witnesses. I was brazenly sipping it from a teacup. Hating where I was with such a passion, such a depthless passion, and passion is an unstoppable thing once it gets going...

The incident itself is a blur. I've pasted it together from what others have told me of course. I don't deny it. I remember the...I suppose you would say, the scuffle. I remember reaching out to her as she passed my desk. And when she winced I turned it into anger. Very easy to do.

I grabbed the cross from her neck, shoving it into her face.

—This is why you're the way you are, I said. This is why you will always be nothing more than a servant. A slave! With this around your neck you'll be a nigger till you die!

Yes. I said that. I did.

Where did that word come from? Who can say? Do I blame it on the H Rider Haggard novels read aloud under the covers to Joan in our freezing flat above the shop? Or on those forgotten pictures flickering above us in that gargantuan cinema? Or on my father's mouth?

No.

All I know is I said it. And worse, I meant it. It sprung from the depths of my vocabulary. Mined by Russian vodka and hate.

THEY WOULDN'T LET ME SEE MY WEE SISTER!

I had let my grip slacken and the woman broke away. She ran. Not to the authorities. But to the papers. And I got what I deserved.

The end.

And yet here I am again, spinning loose and longing to be drunk even though I know...

The desire for it now is overwhelming. It's my desire to be drunk that pulls me up by the strings.

So I'm standing when Rosie appears at the door.

Did she follow me in? Did she sway her way through that horrible mess, unseen, putting her red shoes where mine had been?

But I feel so happy to see her. This strange wee girl that I've only just met and who has said not one word.

I feel like she is my mother, my missing mother here to wipe my tears away and tell me that everything will be alright.

I shake this feeling off. Ridiculous that a woman of my age…

Anyway, I shake it off, and hope that my soaking make-up hasn't made me look like a melting puppet.

I straighten my back, jut my…

No, I don't really have the strength for that.

−Rosie go back to the classroom please, there's a good girl. There's nothing wrong with me, thank you very much, I'm fine.

She doesn't move.

−Look I appreciate that you're worried, but I just needed to… Rosie I am a grown woman and I can look after myself. And whilst it's very sweet that you're worried about me, Mr Ottoway is right, you should be back in the class listening to your lessons and being part of your… ceremony. Rosie I'm alright, please stop looking at me like that!

For a second I think she's going to speak. More than that…

I think she's going to say whatever mystical words have been missing in my life. Comforting words. Guiding words. Reassuring words. The big unsaid. Woman's words. Maybe that's where they've been all this time. Stuck inside this little girl.

I am open. Like a believer waiting on the word of God. My arms are spread…

Say it.

But she doesn't speak. She just points.

Not at me.

But at the cubicle. The toilet cubicle.

And again, one by one, my strings are cut.

She hadn't come to support me, to say some words that I need to hear, or to guide me home. She's six years old and frightened.

She had come to use the toilet.

I bow my head and quickly count to a sad ten.

−Okay Rosie, in here. Use this one.

She pauses, as if unsure.

−Come on girl, in here. I'll stay with you if you need me too.

I don't know why I say it. Unprofessional really, but it's as clear as day to me and the words are right there, so I say…

−Rosie, you don't have devils in you. Or spirits or whatever they say. You're a normal little girl and you will be fine. There's no such thing as devils. There's no such thing as God either. These are just tales that big men have made up to get little girls and boys to do what they want. It's a scary story. That's all. Do you understand me?

She nods in a preoccupied way, as if there's something about this she doesn't get, which of course, there must be.

−In here dear. I'll come in with you, then we'll wash our hands, I'll take you back to the class and I'll disappear. Sounds like a plan doesn't it?

We bundle into the cubicle and lock the door behind us.

Rosie has climbed onto the toilet seat. *Standing*, on the toilet seat.

—No dear, down. That's not how it works.

She puts out her finger and I am silenced. Is this something she picked up from me too or is this just instinctual?

She lifts her skirt. It's a heavy wool hand-me-down. A bigger girl's uniform and she has trouble holding it up. She grips the front folds in her teeth so her hands are free and her pants are showing.

I can't speak.

It seems obscene in some way. Slatternly.

No that's wrong. It feels...like we are a doctor and a patient. Yes. That's it. I've to look for something.

I've to...see.

She pulls down her pants and they catch around her knees. Then she straightens her back. She juts her chin. Her arms fold across her chest and take the weight of the skirt, holding it in place.

And

I do see.

I see what this is about.

I see the source of all that silence.

I see the devil.

And the marks he made on six year old skin.

And then she begins to speak.

***

She finishes by asking me never to tell.

I make my promise.

I will not speak.

We have somehow moved from the cubicle. We are sitting on the tiled floor facing each other. Our legs are crossed like Buddhas. I have both my hands on her shoulders. It looks like I am trying to stop this little girl from flying away. But it's too late for that.

She's very pretty. She'll be a beautiful woman.

When she gets older I'll teach her how to hold herself. How to turn the full beams of her eyes on the men she wants. I'll show her that she can rise above this…this.

I'll show her that she can rise above this.

Together we'll find a man who will see beyond it. If anything it will deepen his love for her. If it's a man that she wants.

She's playing with the rings on my fingers. They are antique. Art Deco design. I hold my hand into the beam of light coming through the frosted glass and let the reflection sparkle the tiles like a mirrorball.

She smiles. Not broadly. But it's a smile. The first smile. In the smile I see her climb back down to being six again. She was ancient for a while there when she spoke. A damaged attic toy. She was venerable. In the Roman Catholic sense. In the way my father would've used the word.

Venerable. She was approaching sanctity.

Why would religion get involved in this? What has skin got to do with them? What has sexual pleasure got to do with them?

What has the skin and the pleasure of a six year old girl got to do with them?

I suppose I must have seen a circumcised man.

I must have. Though I couldn't describe the difference in a court of law.

To me, the penis has always seemed a strange and oddly low status part of sexual relations, regardless what the men say. And on this subject they seem to say a lot. I've had tearful apologies, before and after; boasts, before and after; and even pet names, but I can't *precisely* remember a single one. My lasting impression is that they have never seemed to fit their owner. They look *wrong*. All of them.

I've always had the touch though. The way I cup my hand near the base, the lightness of my fingers and the firmness of my movement, always…*always* had a lightning bolt affect.

But were any of them circumcised? It's possible.

I'll teach her about sex too, when the time is right. I'll show her…I'll show her how to…It's important that she doesn't lose that. It's important that they haven't taken that away. Because that's what they want. That's what they always want.

I give her the ring and she puts it on her finger.

I'll dress her. I'll armour her against the world with her style. I'll educate her. She'll soar through the world.

I'll give her pride. Yes. Pride is what I'll give her.

That hated heirloom will be passed on and maybe now it will do some good. Maybe there'll be a point to it after all?

I am aware too that something is going to happen. Soon. I feel too much to let this pass in a nothing.

Fury. Yes, I think there'll be fury.

But now I feel calm and quiet. I've been taken into her circle of silence and it makes a great deal of sense.

Quiet.

Still.

Yes…that makes sense for the moment.

And

Oh my God

I need a drink. I know that is a deplorable, selfish, ignoble thing at this point, but there you are. I need alcohol to do whatever it is I'm going to do. I need alcohol to do *anything* now. It's a fact. It's a logistical detail.

I need alcohol to get me beyond this.

So while Rosie is momentarily distracted by the beauty of jewellery, my thoughts are with the ugly task of getting to that flask in my bag, currently kicked deep under a desk in a room I can't return to.

And after the alcohol? What then?

I don't know. I don't… Get to the flask and the rest will follow.

And just as I'm wondering how to get from this world into that, the lunch bell rings and I stand as if summoned, take Rosie into my arms and leave that little bathroom forever.

***

My heart's beating and I nearly smile until I remember the severity of this outrage and I pull Rosie tighter against my body, quickening my pace down the hall to the classroom. A controlled, holstered sway is impossible carrying a little girl. But I concentrate on my pace. Not rushing, not panicking. But quick.

Just get to the door.

Get to the bag.

Get to the flask.

We go on. Carefully. Step by step.

There is an exhilaration to this, I know. It's justification.

I am right. They are wrong.

She tightens her grip around my shoulders, giving me ignition as I open the classroom door, justified and looking for trouble.

***

I almost drop Rosie as I bolt for my bag.

But I catch myself. This won't do. She's the reason. So I slow, put her down and straighten.

–Darling, stand there for a minute will you? I just need something from my bag. I'll be two ticks. Then we're going to see what we can do to make everything happy again. Okay? That's it. Stand there dear. Face this way. Here, look through the books. That's it. Good girl.

She goes to the dictionaries and starts to flick. The way she takes my words as gospel etches something hard across my heart.

I reach under the table, grasping for the bag and the flask that will transform this situation and save the day. Where is it? Bloody thing. Come on!

I don't need to turn around to know that someone else has entered the room. There's a pressure change.

–Ah she's here! She's here. Our Rosie. Good, good.

It's whatisname. Wadad. The softness of his voice surprises me. The gears of his pitch have slipped down from pulpit to living room mode. I wonder whether I should find an excuse for being on my knees under a desk.

I've come back for a reason. Haven't I? You have to have a reason to go back.

Yes.

My hands, searching carefully in the bag find what they have been looking for.

It feels like…relief I suppose.

As I stand, I slip it into the pocket of my skirt and it sits there heavily. Can he see it? I don't care.

He's alone.

Guessing my question he says

–The women are looking in the toilets. Mr Ottoway is very upset: Rosie is missing, my goodness! Ha ha. I knew she'd be safe. Our Rosie is a very sensible girl. A clever girl. Right Rosie? Right Nadifa?

I look to Rosie, expecting her to have reverted. To be terrified and sullen. To be cowing and timid in the company of this man. But she looks no different. He is not a horror to her.

It's not as straightforward as that.

He moves towards me and sits on the edge of a desk. He speaks to Rosie without looking at her. His eyes are on me. I can feel the patronising undercurrent cut me with every word he says.

–Perhaps Nadifa you should go next door to Mr Ottoway and wait? He will be glad to see you. He may have some sweets for you. We'll be through in just a moment. I need to have a small word with your teacher. Okay?

She looks to me. I have nothing in response.

But I want her out of here. Away from…this.

–I'll be through in a moment dear. Then we'll…then we'll sort this out. I promise.

Before she goes, she comes close to me. I think for a second she is going to speak again. Would that be the end of it I wonder? Would this all be forgotten if I can prove she is exorcised? That I've banished the demons and brought back her words?

But no, she doesn't speak.

She just places her red shoe next to mine.

Then she turns and walks away.

As herself.

In her own, slow, childish steps.

I should just put my red shoes where hers have been and walk after her. Shouldn't I?

But I don't.

–You think we are barbaric? Miss Brodie? Ignorant I think you said?

What? Oh yes, the shootout…

–I am not a racist.
–No. And I am not necessarily who you think I am either. I am, for instance, a university man. You look surprised?

I can be certain that I do not look surprised. Far from it in fact.

–No. This is how I look when I do not care. I do not care about you. I do not care where you went to university or what you do on a Saturday night. I do however care what you do to six year old girls in the name of religion. And yes, I know. I *know* what you do to six year old girls! And it is, Mr Wadad, barbaric. Oh yes it is.

He shifts slightly. Smiling. Like a politician.

And there is that look from before. A smile that is designed to let me know he is enjoying…no, that he is *titillated*, by my fire.

—Mr Wadad? See...you don't even know my name. And Saturday nights, if you really want to know Miss Brodie, I work. Do you know where I work? You do, you do. I work in Oddbins. Yes. Oddbins. Not far from here. I am interested in wine. The hours are good. They're very forward thinking the staff there. They're very interested in my culture. Very supportive. And I get to see some of their culture in return. Not all of that culture is always so... *cultured,* of course.

To stop the sinking in my stomach I straighten my back and shift onto one hip.

Of course I recognized him. Of course I did.

Sometimes when it's close to ten and I'm still thinking, still *feeling,* and I worry that I don't have enough to last the night, I've been known to...run to...I've been known to run over there. I recognize him from behind the shutters. Pitying me, fascinated at the sight of me shouting gibberish there in my slippers, banging on the glass. Begging.

I recognize him.

But that's not who I am. Not today.

—Don't you dare judge me you...I know you. I know what you did. You may think you know my weakness but I know what you did. She *told* me. The devils were silenced and she spoke. She spoke! She told me! I saw!

I take a lurching step towards him, letting the spin I'm on run its course. Dormant alcohol in my system has been shocked awake and buzzes through my core. Even though the flask remains hidden, I suddenly feel gloriously drunk.

He stands to counter, his palms out. He's putting on a calm, hurt, reasonable act that cuts no ice.

—We...I did not do...*that* to Rosie. You know it okay? Those scars are old. Healed. They're from her home not from here. Not from me. 98% of girls have it done there.

It's a deep, cultural thing. They chose it. She has not been singled out, far from it. They see it as a cleanliness issue, "removing the dirt", a rite of passage. Yes she is too young. Of course. Of course she is. But she's from a very poor part of our country. Very...that is why her family came here in the first place. I am trying to help her now. To bring her into this new world. It's a slow transition process. To teach her, just like you are teaching her, that does not mean...

No, I won't have this! I am not him! I've never been him! We are not the same!

I shove him in the chest and his eyes pop. Shock first and then a confusion. His mouth clicks open but it's my voice that fills the room...

– *You* told her she is possessed by devils! *You* told her that devils are binding tight her lips and turning her words to silence! Devils you said! Devils inside her that made her what she is! Devils that marked *her* out for this treatment and not her sisters! Something like...gelid and wado... waddad...some *nonsense*. That's what you told her! That's your crime!

He would love to hit me. He's pretending to be lost but I know him. I recognize that flush in his eyes and the quickening breath from when he would come stomping in from another angry exchange on the church steps, another unhappy customer cut by trembling scissors, another night spent drinking alone and blaming us for mother leaving...

–These are just words. Just words like "soul" and "angel" and "heaven" and "hell". There's no difference between the words we use and the words Christians use to discuss spirituality...

–Then we agree on something, I say, punching him pathetically on the chest. You're both guilty. All of you! And you'll be punished...punished...in...eh...I mean... you're both...I...I...

I can see my point disappearing in a swirl. His face and my father's, Joan and Rosie, devils and crosses coming together for a second, coherent and focused for a beat then drifting, lost again in my anger and my spin. Confused forever.

I know I can't express it.

I can't.

So I'm right up next to him. Gasping for breath, knowing that the point of this...the *reason* of it all...is forever behind my lips.

I can't speak now. I can't put into words what's so wrong.

And so I can't change anything. I can't make it better.

A promise has been broken.

Somewhere long ago.

A promise has been broken.

And nothing can make that better now.

–I...I...I...

It's been a long time since I've wept. So it feels strange, surprising really, to feel the tears slip down my cheeks.

I make the first move. I always have done.

I wrap my arms around him. And cry.

I lean into his chest. I let the tears come.

Cleaning me. Removing the dirt.

I feel him crane his neck to the door. Can anyone see us? He's confused. We were fighting and now...

I've handed him my confusion.

Then, after a moment, his hands. On my shoulder. On my back.

Yes. This is normal.

This is just what it was like.

It starts as a comforting thing. A man and a girl. Could be a father and a daughter. A pat on the shoulder.

Until the devil in me flares its red and takes over. The movement of me...turns it bad. A shift of my hips. The angle of my hands. An arching in my back.

Where did I get it from? Where did it come from? The devil in me. Some people saw it in my eyes. He saw it. Right from the start.

I lower my shoulders and let my devil out into the room with a sigh.

Its power is incredible. Immediate.

I can feel his belly tighten. He shifts his feet further apart. His touch goes from a stroke to a grip, fingers in my back.

The last part is to turn my full beam on his face, the green light, the "this is okay by me" glint.

A look that says...

Go ahead.

That look...well. That is my crime. Always has been. That is my inescapable. That look. It's undeniable. Isn't it?

Is it?

Maybe I should

Look up.

But when I do. Desperately, desperately look up... It's not him. No.

It's a black man.

It's a strange, sweating, panting black man.

And he's gripping me. Pulling me in, tighter, tighter…

Remember.

Remember Joa…no, Rosie. No what was her real name…?

That's what I've to remember.

As he pulls me into him, his lips on my face, his hand grabbing my skirt like a paw.

And at my hip, I feel it pressing, hard and unstoppable.

My talent. My touch.

Ah yes.

Yes, yes, yes.

That's why it's me! That's why Rosie came to me. Of course. Everything has a pattern. Yes. The stories of our lives are sewn to a pattern that can only be seen at the very, very…very end.

Sewn on a…

Sewn together. Me and her. The good and the bad. For a reason.

Yes.

His tongue is in my mouth now, it tastes of pepper and meat. His eyes are wide open and big, like a baby's, so close to me. This close up all eyes look the same.

I think

She came to me because I have three things.

One:

An ability with men. A skill, a hard earned skill…

I push my left hand under the elastic of his trousers. I cup it near the base, the lightness of my fingers and the firmness of my movement has its usual effect. Electricity. He nearly shouts out but catches himself.

Two:

My father's pride.

My right hand falls low into the holster. And my fingers, moving quickly in the pocket of my skirt, find the wooden handles of The Persuader.

And three:

Unlike everyone I've ever met…I can keep a promise.

***

His scream was…indescribable. Yes. It was an unheard, unreal sound.

The blood too was unreal. It seemed disproportionate. Overdone.

Pouring, pouring, pouring out. Pouring out all over the floor.

The red was released and I was absolutely fascinated by it.

And cured. And cleaned. And convicted by it.

My eyes were on the flooding red when they all charged in.

Everything else was predictable and as you would expect.

The only image in my mind of the time before the police arrived that didn't seem ripped from some hospital drama was Gordon Ottoway charging back through the screaming women in a blood drenched suit carrying a torso full of brittle paper towels.

Perhaps that's what saved the Wadad's life. I don't know. Perhaps his life was never in danger. No-one has ever explained it to me in those terms.

But Rosie wasn't there. Nadifa wasn't there. I looked for her, but she wasn't there.

In the cacophony, as I stood paused, calm, looking for her; I thought that maybe she'd disappeared for good. Maybe what I'd done had vanished her from here, back to that place where she goes to escape. Back to her safe world of quiet for ever.

But of course, no. She was just somewhere else.

And that's the only thing that I regret. There was no last moment. No final goodbye.

But then again there was...

There was the promise. I made her a promise not to tell. And that is all I have now. That is my job. My vocation. That promise is what I do for a living now.

It's all I have.

So far it's not been difficult. I have had only one visitor.

Mr Ottoway...Gordon. He wept. And in my head I took back what I may have thought of him in the past. He's just a gentle wee man really. A broken wee Scottish boy who is getting swept away.

I couldn't work out if he was here to confront me. Or comfort me. Or to abuse me. He did none of those things. He just wept.

I said nothing of course, for the entire visit and watched him weep. He had in his hand a copy of the *Daily Record.*

My face is on the front page. I am a racist. A neo-Nazi. A vicious, disturbed bitch – twisted by hate, I castrate my victims. Race Hate Miss in Immigrant Slash Attack. Apparently I'm the talk of the town.

Such is life.

The fact that this is not what I am like. At all. Is meaningless.

Perhaps in the end that *is* what I'm like. That is, after all, the role I have to play now, until the day I die.

I can presume this is ricocheting on poor Mr Ottoway. He looked like a man in the midst of a catastrophe. His eyes were gritty and raw. His jokes and lightness were a world away.

When he left he said sorry.

Not to me I don't think. He has no reason to say sorry to me. I think he was apologising to Rosie.

And that is a fitting way to see all of this I think. That is, afterall, how I see it.

This is an apology to Rosie.

I am saying sorry. From me to her. From Margaret Ann to Nadifa.

And I will keep my promise. Why? Because she asked me to.

I won't tell.

It's not a sacrifice. I've been looking for something all of my life I suppose. And this is it.

So I will not speak.

I am a match that has been lit. And blown out.

So I will not speak.

And when they come for me, soon, to take me wherever

I'll be fine.

Because I will not speak

I will not speak ever again.

I made her a promise.

I will not speak.

THE END

www.ingramcontent.com/pod-product-compliance
Ingram Content Group UK Ltd.
Pitfield, Milton Keynes, MK11 3LW, UK
UKHW020728280225
455688UK00012B/557